Cost Benefit Jr. ™

Stories in Microeconomics

by Stephanie Herman

for Sam and Nicholas

Table of Contents

Acknowledgements

Grateful appreciation for help with this book is extended to Jordan Goodman, "America's Money Answers Man;" Mark Crowley [Success Radio Show on KNUS-710AM in Denver]; Wayne Jett [Polyconomics]; Linda Gorman [Independence Institute]; Lesley Craig, Cindy Rapp and Roger Barrett [Townsend and Townsend and Crew, LLP]; Kevin Cullis; Jenny Nikaido; Jim and Sara McPeak; Alan Herman; and my inspiration and target audience: Sam and Nicholas Herman. Thank you.

Keira's Allowance

Her first experience with price, cost, and value

Section 1

The Price Is Usually Right

Lesson 1

E-SECRETS the secure, password-protected electronic diary

Price: $12.99

ColorJewel Necklaces
Half off!

Price: $7.99

Betty Bop...
the brunette
with crop-
top style!

Price: $3.99

LAST WEEK, KEIRA OPENED a toy catalog and found three things she really wanted: a Betty Bop doll, a ColorJewel necklace, and an electronic diary. But when she asked her parents to buy them, they suggested – to her surprise – that she start earning an allowance!

So Keira talked with her parents about the jobs she might do each week to earn this money. Eventually it was decided that she would feed the cat, make her bed, and put away her folded clothes. If she did all her chores each week, her parents would pay Keira $2.50 every Friday.

After doing these jobs for a week, Keira was impressed at how *productive* she'd been! Her cat was well-fed, her bed was neat, her clothes were unwrinkled, and she was responsible for those good things happening. Keira was proud of the work she had done – her cleaning and cat-feeding and laundry **PRODUCTION** – and she felt good about herself for accomplishing that.

Production can mean making new things, helping other people, cleaning up messes, growing vegetables, fixing bicycles, baking a cake... production can be any activity that makes your life or the lives of other people *better!*

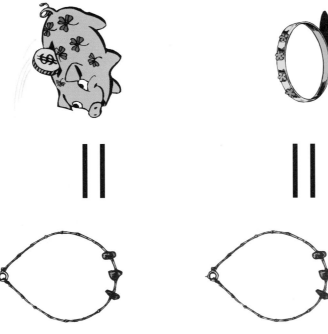

In economics, though, production not only means activities that make life better, but that are also *valuable* to other people. Production that someone else needs or wants can be exchanged for money! In Keira's case, her cleaning production and cat-feeding production were exchanged every week for $2.50, because Keira's productive work around the house was worth that much money to her parents.

After three weeks, Keira had earned a total of $7.50, so she looked up the three items in the catalog that she really wanted to buy. Keira had only earned enough allowance money to afford the Betty Bop doll. If she wanted either the necklace or the diary, she would have to earn more money.

But then, she remembered that her friend, Terese, had a ColorJewel necklace that she no longer wanted. It wasn't new, of course, but Terese would be willing to trade Keira the necklace for a ring in Keira's jewelry box that she never wore. This ring was an **ASSET**, something of value that you own.

Now, if Keira bought the necklace from the catalog, its price would equal $7.99, but if she traded with Terese, the price of the necklace would equal one old ring.

Which price, she wondered, am I more willing to pay?

Giving Terese her old ring meant Keira could have the necklace without spending her allowance. This would leave her allowance money for either the doll or the diary. Keira made her choice: she traded her ring for Terese's necklace.

By trading their jewelry, the girls made an economic exchange of **GOODS** – tangible products we can touch or hold. Keira bought the ColorJewel necklace for a price both could agree on, a *fair* price. We say that an economic exchange is fair when both the buyer and seller *benefit* from the exchange. And a price is fair when both the buyer and seller agree on that price. These aspects of fairness can exist when people are free to choose what's best for them in the marketplace – in a *"free-market"* economy.

Now, prices are usually paid with money, but sometimes – in a trade or **BARTER** – the price is paid with an asset, like Keira's old ring. Keira and Terese are free to barter, and they must agree on what's fair.

After trading with Terese, Keira felt she had made a good choice. Now she just needed to stay productive and enjoy the benefits: earning enough allowance money for the electronic diary!

Mr. Greedy L. McMeanie

Mr. Greedy L. McMeanie doesn't understand free markets. He doesn't care if his customers benefit; he wants to charge us more than he should. Luckily, market forces can stop Mr. McMeanie! If we don't benefit from doing business with him, we'll take our business, and our money, somewhere else. We won't <u>agree to</u> the exchange! That's the power of consumer choice. Capitalism provides many market forces like consumer choice to keep Mr. McMeanie from hurting us economically. But it's up to us to know what those market forces are, and how to use them!

Quick Quiz

Lesson 1

1. What are the two prices Keira could have paid for the ColorJewel necklace?

    1.

        or

    2.

2. Which price was Keira more willing to pay?

3. What is production?
    a. a product in a store
    b. an organization that helps ducks
    c. work that has value to others

4. Circle the term that best describes an exchange of goods without money:
    a. allowance
    b. barter
    c. price

5. What is an asset?

6. An economic exchange is fair when both the buyer and seller _____ from the exchange. A price is fair when both the buyer and seller _____ on that price.

Next Best

Lesson 2

THREE WEEKS LATER, KEIRA had earned a total of $15 in allowance money. Once again, she pulled out her store catalog and looked up the E-Secrets secure, password-protected electronic diary. The price was still $12.99 and Keira was willing to pay it. She chose a color and read about all the features – diary fonts and friendship lists and a school-day planner.

And just as she was about to ask her mom to place the order, she looked again at the Betty Bop doll in all her crop-topped glory… and paused.

Betty Bop came with a set of crop-top outfits in three different colors, and you could buy her a pair of red sneakers (sold separately). Her hair looked cute in a ponytail and all of Keira's friends carried one of these dolls in their backpacks. Keira had waited weeks to get a Betty Bop doll and she could have it – right now – if she weren't already buying the diary.

She suddenly realized that the E-Secrets secure, password-protected electronic diary wouldn't just cost her $12.99 – it would also cost her the opportunity to buy that cute little doll that all her friends had. $12.99 may have been the price-cost of the diary, but the Betty Bop doll – the next best choice – was the **OPPORTUNITY COST** of the diary.

An opportunity cost shows up any time you choose one thing over another – the next best thing not chosen is a missed opportunity, a cost to you. That's why we often say we pick one thing at the expense of something else – an expense is like a cost.

Now Keira was faced with a difficult choice. The diary or the doll? The doll or the diary? She fell on her bed in a flop of frustration. Which did she want more? Oh, she wanted them equally. Well then, which did she want sooner? Hm. She wanted the doll before summer, certainly, but her family's vacation was coming up in a few weeks and she really wanted a diary to record all the fun things she'd be doing at Large Lake.

That settled it. Her *first* choice was the diary, and the *next-best choice* would be the doll. So she would buy the diary now, at the expense of buying the doll.

Quick Quiz

Lesson 2

1. How do we know that the price of the electronic diary was the right price for Keira?

2. What are the two costs Keira must pay for the diary?

   1.

      and

   2.

3. What do we call giving up the next-best thing when making a choice?

4. Have you ever bought an item at the expense of buying something else? If so, what was the item you bought, and what was your opportunity cost?

Family "Values"

Lesson 3

BEFORE LONG, KEIRA'S BROTHER Sam discovered that she now had an E-Secrets secure, password-protected electronic diary stashed in her bedside drawer. He snuck into her bedroom one afternoon, snatched the diary, and fiddled with the buttons. When Keira found him there, trying to read her diary, she had only one thing to say.

"Mother!"

Once Mom was brought into the situation, it was quickly decided that Sam needed something better to read than Keira's diary. So the three of them piled into the van and drove to the library.

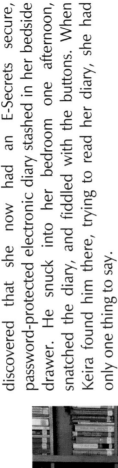

"Here." Keira handed Sam a book on model airplanes.

"Maybe this will keep you out of my room."

Sam shook his head. "I have that book at home."

"You do? But why..." Keira frowned. "Why would you *buy* this book when you could check it out from the library for free?"

To answer Keira's question, we need to understand how people place **VALUE** on things. One person might only value the book on model airplanes for the information inside. That person could read the library book and return it; he's satisfied with reading it just once. Another person, like Sam, might prefer to own the book so he can read it again, whenever he wants.

11

A product's value, then, is its worth to you and me, and that worth will vary. Everyone's needs and wants are different, and we all seek out different products to satisfy them. When a product is useful or desirable to Sam, we say it has **UTILITY** for Sam – it satisfies a want or a need. And if a product satisfies the wants or needs of people, then we say the product is *valuable* to them.

Back at home, Keira saw Sam's copy of the book on model airplanes. She opened it up and read the Table of Contents.

"How boring," she thought. To Keira, this book held no value – it wouldn't be worth any amount of money to her. But to Sam, the book did hold value. It satisfied his desire to know more about models and kits, about the physics of lift and thrust, and the performance of various model airplane styles. And it satisfied his desire to be able to re-read this information whenever he wanted.

The very same product can be valued differently by different people. This is because value is **SUBJECTIVE**; it varies from person to person. Sam's book held a value of $0 to Keira, but a value of at least $6.95 to Sam because that's what he was willing to pay for it.

If he hadn't valued the book at $6.95 – if he thought that price was too high – he would have had two choices: negotiate a different price from the bookseller or refuse to buy the book. In a free market, Sam always has *choices*. As it turned out, Sam agreed to the price and now he owns the book he wanted.

Quick Quiz

Lesson 3

1. Do people always place the same value on a product?

2. If a product satisfies a girl's wants or needs, then that product has _____ for her. (The same is true for boys!)

3. Because any product's value varies from person to person, we say that value is:
   a. objective
   b. subjective
   c. universal

4. What value, in dollars and cents, did Sam place on the model airplane book?

5. What value, in dollars and cents, did Keira place on the model airplane book?

6. How do we know that Sam felt the book's price was fair?

Section 1 Wrap-Up

Lesson 4

Do you get an allowance? If you do, fill out the chart below.
(If you don't, fill out the chart pretending that you get $2.00 per week.)

Amount of allowance I receive every week: $ _____

Chores I do in exchange for my allowance money:

1.

2.

3.

Wish list of items I hope to buy with my allowance money:

1.   Price: $ _____

2.   Price: $ _____

3.   Price: $ _____

Section 1 Wrap-Up, con't.

Lesson 4

1. How many weeks of chores will it take you to save up for the least expensive item?

2. How many weeks of chores will it take you to save up for the most expensive item?

3. Which item on your list is your first choice?

4. What might you give up as an opportunity cost to buy your first choice?

Section 1 Matching

Lesson 4

Match the following terms with the correct definitions:

Fair Price ☐   ☐ next-best item we give up when making a choice

Production ☐   ☐ worth of goods or services

Subjective Value ☐   ☐ work that has value to others

Exchange ☐   ☐ value that varies from person to person

Opportunity Cost ☐   ☐ satisfaction of a want or need

Utility ☐   ☐ price agreed upon by the seller and buyer

Value ☐   ☐ giving in return for receiving

How Much is that Froggy?

How supply & demand determine price

Section 2

Willing and Able

Lesson 5

KEIRA WAS HAPPY WITH HER PURCHASE of the E-Secrets diary. It had utility for Keira (it satisfied her wants or needs). She was willing to pay its price. Because she both wanted to buy it and was able to buy it, we can say that Keira expressed **DEMAND** for the E-Secrets diary.

Of course, there also had to be a **SUPPLY** at the catalog warehouse. Without a supply of E-Secrets diaries, Keira's demand would go unmet. Supply and demand are "partners" working together in every economic exchange.

Starting with extremely simple definitions, supply would mean "available goods" and demand would mean "desire or need for the goods." Using these simple definitions, we can find examples of supply and demand in our everyday lives, like a school of fish and a boy with a fishing pole…

Supply

Demand

Or the corner fruit stand and a hungry little girl...

Demand

Supply

Or shelves of cowboy boots and six pairs of bare feet!

Demand

Supply

19

In economics, however, these simple definitions don't tell the whole story. Economic demand for any given product or service is actually made up of two things: 1) *willingness* to buy, and 2) *ability* to buy.

Likewise, economic supply is the amount of a product or service the producer 1) is *willing* to sell, and 2) is *able* to sell. The key is being both <u>willing</u> and <u>able</u>!

Jean-Baptiste Say

So how does a girl like Keira have the ability to supply something? Well, as we read earlier, she can supply her own hard work, her production. That is, she can supply it if she's both <u>willing</u> to work and <u>able</u> to work. We can look at the act of "supplying" as simply being productive. And once Keira earns money from her production, she can express demand for goods like the Betty Bop doll and the electronic diary!

The idea that supply (our own productive work) can create demand (our ability to buy something) was stated as an economic law by a French economist named Jean-Baptiste Say. It eventually became known as **SAY'S LAW**: *supply creates its own demand.* Keira might re-word Say's Law as: *doing my chores lets me buy a diary.*

20

When we demand goods, being both willing and able is key. For example, Keira may truly want, with all her heart, to buy a pink-saddled show pony. But without $15,000, a barn in the backyard, and her parents' permission, she doesn't come close to having the <u>ability</u> to buy one.

On the other hand, Keira may have the ability to buy Sam's book on model airplanes (once she's saved up $6.95 in her allowance). But as we know, she's not <u>willing</u> to buy that book.

Keira doesn't express economic demand for the show pony because she can't (she's not <u>able</u>). She doesn't express economic demand for the model-airplane book because she won't (she's not <u>willing</u>). But because she was willing and able to buy the E-Secrets diary, she expressed real economic demand for it!

Quick Quiz

Lesson 5

1. Supply is:
   a. the amount of goods or services someone is willing to produce
   b. the amount of goods or services someone is able to produce
   c. both a and b

2. Demand is:
   a. the customer's willingness to buy
   b. the customer's ability to buy
   c. both a and b

3. The idea that "supply creates its own demand" is known as _____ Law.

4. If you really want to buy an ice cream cone (you're willing) but you don't have enough money (you're not able), can you express economic demand for the ice cream cone?

5. On a separate sheet of paper, draw your own example of Supply and Demand.

What We'll Consume

MR. GOAD GROWS grapes for the wine and produce industries in his hometown. Sam and Keira love to visit Goad's Vineyard in the summer. He sells his fresh, juicy grapes to all his friends and neighbors for $1.49 per pound.

Is that a fair price? Probably so, because most of Mr. Goad's friends and neighbors are willing to pay it. But how did Mr. Goad know what to charge? Believe it or not, he let his customers help him figure it out!

This is how he did it. First, Mr. Goad had to

figure out how much it cost to produce the grapes. He can't sell them for *less* than it costs him; he would lose money! It costs 94 cents per pound to grow his grapes, so 94 cents is the lowest price he could charge.

Next, Mr. Goad had to understand the **LAW OF DEMAND**: *at higher prices customers buy less; at lower prices they buy more.* So he began experimenting to see how many grapes his customers would buy at various prices above 94 cents.

← **Vertical Axis**

Horizontal Axis ←

Mr. Goad started by making a graph. He put the prices he charged on the <u>vertical axis</u> (the line going up and down) and the quantities of grapes his customers demanded (or bought) on the <u>horizontal axis</u> (the line running side to side).

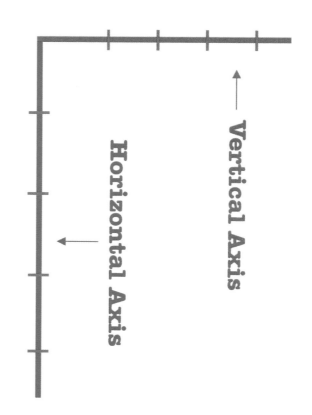

**Price of grapes
(per pound)**

$1.69

$1.09

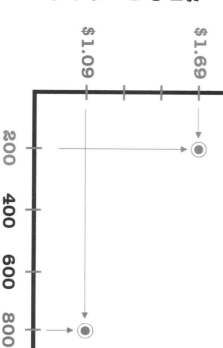

200 400 600 800

**Pounds of
grapes demanded**

Then, Mr. Goad tried charging different prices. At $1.69, he only sold 200 pounds, but at $1.09 he sold 800 pounds! His customers were waiting in line to buy his grapes at that price!

On his graph, he placed two dots that lined up with these prices on the vertical axis and the quantity of grapes demanded on the horizontal axis.

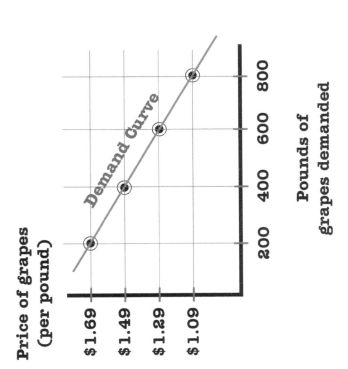

Price of grapes (per pound)

$1.69
$1.49
$1.29
$1.09

Demand Curve

200 400 600 800

Pounds of grapes demanded

At 800 pounds demanded, though, Mr. Goad had a problem. It was very hard to produce *that* many grapes. It took a lot of extra work and he had to hire Bill, a part-time employee. Paying wages to Bill meant that it cost more to produce the grapes: not 94 cents, but $1.21 per pound. Since he was only charging $1.09, Mr. Goad was losing money! Because of this, he was neither willing nor <u>able</u> to supply 800 pounds.

After that, Mr. Goad tried some other prices. He found the quantity demanded at $1.29 was 600 pounds, and at $1.49, the quantity demanded was 400 pounds. He plotted these points on his graph.

When he drew a line through all the dots, he saw his **DEMAND CURVE**. (It's called a curve, even if it's a straight line.) He could now place a dot anywhere on the demand curve and pretty well know how many grapes would be demanded (or bought) at each price!

Quick Quiz

Lesson 6

1. Write down the **LAW OF DEMAND** (look on page 23):

_____

2. Circle the correct word: On a graph, the prices are shown on the **VERTICAL** / **HORIZONTAL** axis.

3. Circle the correct word: On a graph, the quantity demanded is shown on the **VERTICAL** / **HORIZONTAL** axis.

4. Based on this graph, how many pounds of grapes are Mr. Goad's customers willing and able to buy at the price of $1.29? (Plot the dot on the demand curve.)

_____ pounds

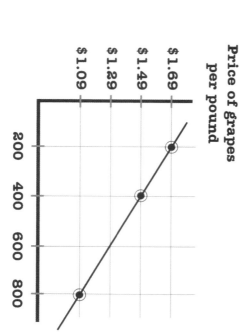

Price of grapes per pound

$1.69
$1.49
$1.29
$1.09

200 400 600 800

Pounds of grapes demanded

What We'll Produce

Lesson 7

AFTER MR. GOAD HAD SUPPLIED different amounts of grapes for different prices, he started to plot his **SUPPLY CURVE.**

While the demand curve told him how many pounds of grapes customers would <u>demand</u> at various prices, the supply curve will tell him how many pounds of grapes he can <u>supply</u> at various prices. The **LAW OF SUPPLY** tells Mr. Goad that: *at higher prices more products are supplied; at lower prices, fewer products are supplied.*

Based on his experiments, Mr. Goad felt that 400 pounds of grapes was a reasonable amount to grow, tend, and harvest in one summer. At a price of $1.49 Mr. Goad was both willing and able to supply 400 pounds of grapes, so he put that dot on his graph.

Then he thought about the lowest price he had charged: $1.09 per pound. At that price, he wouldn't make very much money per pound. He was only willing to sell 200 pounds at that price – maybe to his relatives or the kind old lady who lived next door. So he plotted another dot to line up with $1.09 on the vertical axis and 200 pounds on the horizontal axis. With two dots plotted, he could draw a line through them to see his supply curve.

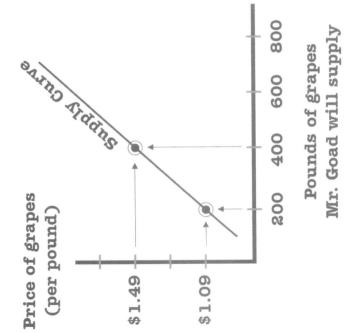

27

Price of grapes
(per pound)

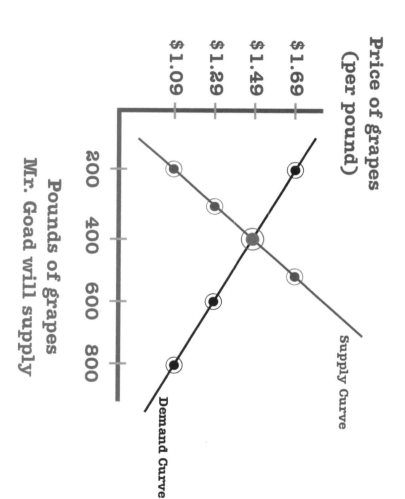

$1.69

$1.49

$1.29

$1.09

Supply Curve

Demand Curve

200 400 600 800

Pounds of grapes
Mr. Goad will supply

When Mr. Goad put his supply curve and his demand curve on the graph together, he found that they met, or intersected, at one point.

28

The demand curve represents what his customers are willing and able to buy, and the supply curve represents what Mr. Goad is willing and able to sell. So the point at which these two curves intersect is where Mr. Goad and the largest number of his customers will agree on the price! In this case, the curves intersect at $1.49 per pound, so Mr. Goad knows that's a fair price!

Mr. Greedy L. McMeanie

Mr. Greedy L. McMeanie still doesn't understand free markets. He picked a price that's way too high, just so he could make more money! Luckily, market forces can stop Mr. McMeanie. If he chooses a price on his supply curve that never intersects with his demand curve, he won't make any money, and he'll soon be out of business. That's the power of supply and demand. Capitalism provides many market forces like supply and demand to keep Mr. McMeanie from hurting us economically. But remember: it's up to us to know what those market forces are, and how to use them!

Quick Quiz

Lesson 7

1. Based on this graph, how many pounds of grapes is Mr. Goad willing and able to supply at the price of $1.29? (Plot the dot on the supply curve.)

_____ pounds

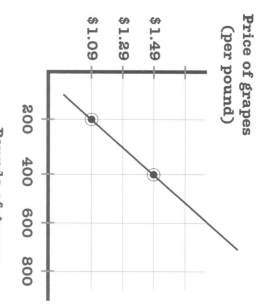

**Price of grapes
(per pound)**

$1.49
$1.29
$1.09

200 400 600 800

**Pounds of grapes
Mr. Goad will supply**

2. Write down the **LAW OF SUPPLY** (look on page 27):

3. The supply curve shows what Mr. Goad is willing and able to _____ at various prices.

4. Where supply and demand curves meet is where Mr. Goad and the largest number of his customers will _____ on the price!

Demand vs. Quantity Demanded

Lesson 8

SAM AND KEIRA SAT ON Mr. Goad's porch eating the grapes they bought. Mr. Goad sat with them, listening to Sam's big plan. He was going into business – Sam wanted to make and sell frog habitats.

He'd start with a plastic container, then furnish it with all the stuff a pet frog might need: a rock to sit on, a tiny pond, plastic lily pads, etc.

Sam was wondering what to charge for each frog habitat, and Mr. Goad had just explained how supply and demand help you determine the right price.

"So according to the Law of Demand," Sam said, "if I lower my price, I'll increase demand."

"Well, no," Mr. Goad shook his head.

"What?" Keira asked. "I thought you said that at lower prices, people will buy more!"

"A lower price increases the **QUANTITY DEMANDED**, not the *demand*," Mr. Goad told them. "There's a big difference between the two." Sam and Keira looked confused, so Mr. Goad explained by telling them more about his grape business.

"The demand for grapes is based on many things, like how much money my customers earn at work, how hungry they are, and how much they like the taste of grapes. The one thing that doesn't change the demand for grapes is the *price*.

"You see," he continued, "if I lower my price, my customers will buy more grapes. That's a change in the amount sold – the *quantity demanded*. But the things that create *demand* don't change just because I raise or lower my price. You don't like the taste of grapes less when they're priced higher do you?"

Sam and Keira laughed. "No, we like the taste of grapes no matter what they cost."

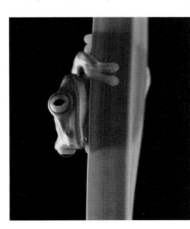

31

"And my price doesn't change how much money my customers like grapes or how hungry they are. My price only changes the amount people will buy – people who were going to buy grapes anyway."

Here's the difference, shown on the graph: when a price changes, so does the position of the dot on a demand curve. It moves up and down on that curve. This is a change in *quantity demanded*.

Change in Quantity Demanded

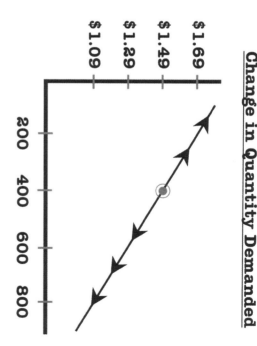

$1.69
$1.49
$1.29
$1.09

200 400 600 800

Change in Demand

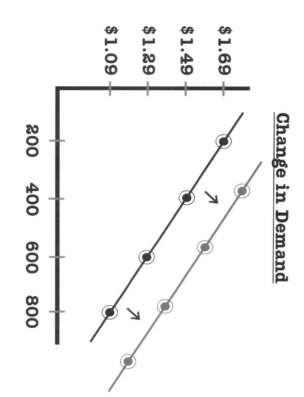

$1.69
$1.49
$1.29
$1.09

200 400 600 800

But when *demand* itself changes, including things like how much money customers earn and what their tastes are, the whole demand curve shifts.

"Oh, I get it!" Sam piped up. "If I lower the price of my frog habitats, I increase how many habitats will be bought by the boys who already want them (the quantity demanded). But for *demand* of my habitats to increase, something else needs to happen, like all the girls suddenly wanting pet frogs!"

"Well, that's pretty unlikely," Mr. Goad laughed. "But yes, I think you get the idea."

Quick Quiz

Lesson 8

1. A lower price increases:
   a. demand
   b. quantity demanded

2. For Mr. Goad's grapes, factors like their tastes in food would change the:
   a. demand
   b. quantity demanded

3. A change in demand would result in the following change on a graph:
   a. the demand curve would shift
   b. the dot on a demand curve would move up or down

4. A change in quantity demanded would result in the following change on a graph:
   a. the demand curve would shift
   b. the dot on a demand curve would move up or down

Supply vs. Quantity Supplied

WE'VE LEARNED HOW SUPPLY

and demand help determine the price of goods, which are tangible products. But how do supply and demand apply to **SERVICES**, which are *intangible* products?

Sam's friend Nicholas runs a dog-walking business. He doesn't sell anything tangible: dog-walking is a service. So how can we measure the "supply" of a service?

He was able to measure his dog-walking supply by timing how long it takes him to walk a dog – about 15 minutes. It also takes time to walk from one house to another between jobs, so he added five minutes to each job. Since he could work no more than an hour after school (and still get his homework done), he figured that he could do three 20-minute jobs per day.

Nicholas is neither willing nor able to supply more than three walks a day. And he knows the **LAW OF SUPPLY:** *at higher prices more products are supplied, and at lower prices fewer are supplied.* So he's plotted a supply curve to show his willingness and ability to perform one, two, and three jobs a day, based on the price.

Price

$1.00
$0.75
$0.50

Dog-walks supplied per day

1 2 3

As with demand, we know that changes can occur in both **SUPPLY** and **QUANTITY SUPPLIED**. His supply of dog-walks is based on the fact that he enjoys walking dogs. The one thing that does *not* change his supply of dog-walks is the *price*. In other words, even if a neighbor offered him $5 to do a fourth walk after school, he wouldn't have the time and his mother wouldn't let him. Higher prices don't increase supply or the amount of time Nicholas can spend at work.

What would change his supply? Well, during the summer he likes to travel with his family, and that can affect both his willingness and ability to supply his service. Less time at home means he is less able to work, and his entire supply curve would shift.

On the other hand, it's his *quantity supplied* that changes when he raises or lowers his price. He's more willing to do all three dog-walks after school if he's being paid well ($1.00 per walk). If he only stands to make 50 cents on a dog walk, he'd rather just walk one dog and free up the rest of his time to play baseball!

Change in Supply

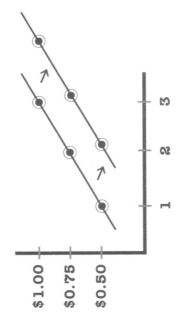

Change in Quantity Supplied

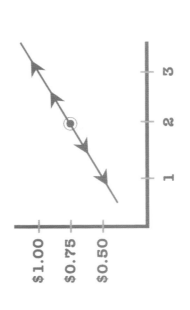

Quick Quiz

Lesson 9

1. A higher price increases:
   a. supply
   b. quantity supplied

2. For Nicholas' dog-walking service, factors like how much he likes dogs would affect the:
   a. supply
   b. quantity supplied

3. A change in <u>supply</u> would result in the following change on a graph:
   a. the supply curve would shift
   b. the dot on a supply curve would move up or down

4. A change in <u>quantity supplied</u> would result in the following change on a graph:
   a. the supply curve would shift
   b. the dot on a supply curve would move up or down

5. Circle the correct words: We call tangible products **GOODS / SERVICES** and we call intangible products **GOODS / SERVICES**.

Section 2 Wrap-Up

Lesson 10

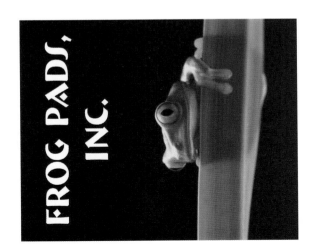

FROG PADS, INC.

Pretend you're the owner of Frog Pads, Incorporated. Use the graph to answer the questions below.

1. Your first year in business, you charge $9.50 each for your frog habitats. At this price, your company sells 5000 habitats. Plot a dot for this price and quantity demanded.

2. Your second year in business you charge $7.50 each for your frog habitats. At this price, your company sells 7000 habitats. Plot a dot for this price and quantity demanded.

3. Draw a line through your dots to see the demand curve.

Price of each frog habitat

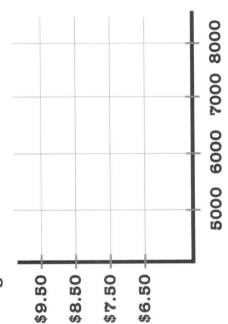

$9.50

$8.50

$7.50

$6.50

5000 6000 7000 8000

Frog habitats demanded

Section 2 Wrap-Up, con't.

Lesson 10

4. Using the demand curve, can you predict how many habitats your company will sell if you charge $6.50 each?

5. Using the demand curve, what price should your company charge to sell 6000 habitats?

Section 2 Matching

Lesson 10

Match the following terms with the correct definitions:

Supply ☐

Demand ☐

Quantity Demanded ☐

Quantity Supplied ☐

Tangible ☐

Horizontal Axis ☐

Vertical Axis ☐

☐ amount of goods or services customers are willing & able to buy at a specific price

☐ goods or services someone is willing & able to produce

☐ axis of a graph running side to side

☐ customers' willingness and ability to buy

☐ axis of a graph going up and down

☐ amount of goods/services someone is willing & able to produce at a specific price

☐ something you can touch or hold

Cost Benefit Jr.™

Big Rewards

People respond to incentives

Section 3

41

The Cost of Watching TV

Lesson 11

ERICA DOESN'T USUALLY SPEND time with her little brother. He's too loud, too destructive, and too into football. But lately, Erica has been watching a TV show every day with her brother. It features home videotapes of funny animals and crazy pets. Believe it or not, it's the only activity Erica and her brother can enjoy together!

Erica is also learning to play the guitar. She's supposed to practice one half-hour every day in order to learn a pretty little song called, "Day at the River."

It's an easy song, lovely and melodic, but it will take some practice to master it, to play it without mistakes. If Erica can show her teacher that she's mastered "Day at the River," she'll be able to play it in the spring recital!

Erica has dreamed of performing in the recital. She's always wanted to play beautiful music in front of an audience. She wants to make people happy! She also wants to hear the applause. But she can't play in the recital unless she completes her task of learning and mastering "Day at the River."

Playing in the recital, the beautiful music, the applause, are all **INCENTIVES** motivating Erica to complete her task. Incentives can encourage us to act or discourage us from acting. These specific incentives encourage Erica to act in a specific way: to practice her guitar.

An incentive can be either negative or positive. A negative incentive like prison can discourage us from the act of stealing. A soccer trophy is a positive incentive – it can encourage us to play harder and better, actions we hope will win us the trophy.

In economics, we call negative incentives our "costs." If I steal someone's car I might end up paying a cost: going to prison. On the other hand, we call positive incentives our "benefits." If I play hard in the game today I might be gaining a trophy to take home. Most of the time we behave or act in ways that will benefit us. And in a free market, we can choose to buy and sell when it benefits us.

Now, Erica is very excited about the spring recital, but at a recent guitar lesson she was still making mistakes when she played "Day at the River." Her teacher wasn't sure she'd be ready to perform in the recital. Erica was crushed.

She had to admit, though, that it was her own fault. She hadn't been practicing a half-hour every day because she'd been watching TV, instead. She just loved the segments on cats and kittens. They were so cute, and cuddly, and fluffy, and funny! It always seems like a good idea to sit down and watch this show, but Erica has paid a high price for watching TV.

Remember, every action we choose comes with an **OPPORTUNITY COST**: the next-best option you give up when making a choice. Watching TV isn't just a break, or time-out from your life. It's an active choice with an opportunity cost.

So what was Erica's next-best choice? In this case, it was practicing her guitar – the most valuable option she gave up to watch TV. Still, even when she plays her guitar, she pays an opportunity cost. Sometimes that opportunity cost is playing with friends; sometimes it's reading a book; sometimes it's riding her bike. But it's never all three: an opportunity cost is only the most valuable thing you give up when making a choice. We always pay just one opportunity cost.

So Erica must choose which opportunity cost she's willing to pay, and when. Once she realized this, she discovered that the benefit of playing the guitar well was worth more to her than the benefit of watching TV. That meant that watching TV was not *really* her first choice! When you pick your second choice rather than your first choice, you've made a *bad* choice.

Luckily, Erica started making better choices. She practiced extra hours and was able to master "Day at the River." She still made a mistake here and there, but her teacher knew that mastery doesn't mean perfection. He decided she was ready to perform in front of an audience and was proud of how hard she worked to catch up!

The night of the recital, her parents and brother sat in the front row. Erica was surprised that, as she walked on stage, she felt nervous! Her stomach fluttered and she didn't want to look out into the audience.

She sat down and cautiously started to play "Day at the River." The first few notes sounded nice, so she continued, gaining confidence. She focused her mind, then relaxed, and her hand found its way through the song's difficult fingering. When she was finished, a few people, including her family, started to clap. More people joined in, and Erica got to experience something she'd always wanted: making an audience happy. In return, they paid her back with a wonderful sound of their own: applause.

Quick Quiz

Lesson 11

1. What was Erica's main incentive to learn and master "Day at the River"?

2. What do we call a "positive incentive" and a "negative incentive"?

3. How many opportunity costs do you pay when making a choice?

   a. only one
   b. more than five
   c. an infinite amount

4. What is the opportunity cost Erica paid for watching TV?

5. Do we ever watch TV without paying a cost?

A Cost-Benefit Analysis

Lesson 12

THE STUDY OF ECONOMICS is really just looking at the reasons why people take action. Ludwig von Mises was an economist in the early 20th century who noticed that people only take action when they feel uneasy about something. We usually don't eat, for example, without first feeling hungry. When we're hungry, we're not content; we are uneasy until we take action (eat) and satisfy our hunger.

So how do people decide whether or not to take action? It's pretty easy: they must think about the costs and *benefits* of taking action. We call this type of thinking a "cost-benefit-analysis."

Nobody does anything (takes action) without first judging their incentives. Hunger is an incentive to eat. Sometimes, we're too busy playing and don't want to stop to eat – a fun game can be an incentive not to eat. So we judge our level of hunger, and when it's high enough that it *outweighs* the cost of stopping our game, we eat!

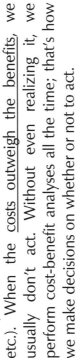

Judging incentives is another way of saying we analyze the costs and benefits. When the benefits outweigh the costs, we usually act (eat, buy, sell, etc.). When the costs outweigh the benefits, we usually don't act. Without even realizing it, we perform cost-benefit analyses all the time; that's how we make decisions on whether or not to act.

When Keira chose to buy the electronic diary rather than the Betty Bop doll, she looked at her incentives – she did a cost-benefit analysis. Her costs were 1) the price of the diary, and 2) not buying the doll. Both costs meant less to Keira than the benefit of owning an electronic diary to record her vacation experiences.

But sometimes costs are too high. The $15,000 price tag for a pink-saddled show pony is a cost that far outweighs the benefit to Keira of owning a small horse.

What will you do today? What actions will you take? Chances are high that you will make an economic calculation in your head before you decide to do anything!

Quick Quiz

Lesson 12

1. People only take action when they feel _____.

2. Positive incentives are also known as _____.

3. Negative incentives are also known as _____

_____.

4. What do we call the process of judging incentives?

The Stray Dog

Lesson 13

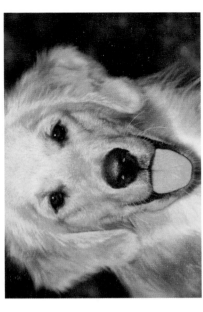

MARLA WAS ALWAYS a cat person. That is, until one day when a stray dog fell asleep on her porch!

When she found him there, she woke him up and offered him a bite of cheese. His happy face looked up into hers, and he tilted his head as if to say, "Thank you." That was all it took: Marla was in love. "I'll call you Mopsy," she told him, and went to ask her dad if she could keep the big yellow dog.

Her father wasn't against the idea, but he wanted Marla to make an informed decision. He wanted her to look at all sides of dog ownership before trying it, herself.

"OK," Marla agreed, and while her dad called the pound to see if the dog was reported as lost, Marla set to work on a cost-benefit analysis:

Benefits of owning a dog

Love and companionship
Dog walks are fun!
Dogs protect the family

Costs of owning a dog

Feeding him every day
Walking him every day
Cleaning up his messes
Paying for food and vet bills

She had to be honest – her parents would be paying the cost of dog food and vet bills. But she could pay the costs of feeding and walking the dog – and maybe she and her mother could split the cost of cleaning up his messes!

Still, she could only come up with three benefits, while there were at least four costs. She racked her brain to think of more benefits, but couldn't, and finally had to give up and show the list to her dad.

"Tell me," he said, after reading the list, "does the love of a dog outweigh all these costs?"

Marla thought about it. "You know, it really does." She realized that one benefit – if it's important enough – can outweigh many costs.

Marla's father suggested that she assign number values to each cost and benefit. This would help her see how one important benefit could outweigh several smaller costs.

Costs of owning a dog

Feeding him every day [2]
Walking him every day [1]
Cleaning up his messes [8]
Paying for food and vet bills [5]

Total Cost Value: 16

Benefits of owning a dog

Love and companionship [10]
Dog walks are fun! [7]
Dogs protect the family [2]

Total Benefit Value: 19

Based on the number values, Marla could see that the costs, however high, were still *lower* than the benefits.

So her dad let her keep the dog, and Marla was a great dog owner. She faithfully fed and walked Mopsy, and even taught him some tricks. Cleaning his messes was an awful job, though – it was a high price to pay. But Marla had agreed to pay that price, and in exchange for her hard work she had the love and companionship of a very loyal dog.

Mr. Greedy L. McMeanie

Mr. Greedy L. McMeanie doesn't understand cost benefit analysis. He sees only that being fair to his customers costs him some money, time, and effort. He doesn't see the benefits of customer esteem and loyalty that he would get in return. That's the power of cost benefit analysis -- it lets us see that even when we pay costs, sometimes we reap even <u>more</u> benefits. Until Mr. McMeanie sees both the costs and benefits of his actions, he'll keep making the same mistakes and it will take him longer to build good relationships with the customers in his community.

Quick Quiz

Lesson 13

1. In a cost-benefit analysis, do you need more benefits than costs in order to take the action?

2. Can one cost, if it's important enough, outweigh many benefits?

3. Just listing costs and benefits isn't enough to analyze if something is more costly or more beneficial. What can we add to the cost-benefit analysis to see if costs are higher or benefits are higher?

4. Do you think Marla was more likely to clean up Mopsy's messes willingly and with fewer complaints since she agreed to them up front in her cost-benefit analysis?

Profit: A Really Big Incentive

Lesson 14

LORI WANTS TO BUY A NEW bicycle, but she doesn't have enough money. So she's decided to set up a lemonade stand in hopes of earning some. Because she's taking the risk of starting her own business, we call Lori an **ENTREPRENEUR**.

Lori's choice to become an entrepreneur was based on two incentives. The first incentive, a positive incentive, was the opportunity to make a **PROFIT**. A profit is your **REVENUE** (money you receive selling goods or services) minus your **PRODUCTION COSTS** (what it costs to produce your goods or services).

Revenue - Production Costs = Profit

So if it costs Lori 12 cents to produce a glass of lemonade and she sells that glass of lemonade for 50 cents, she earns a profit of 38 cents.

50¢ - **12¢** = **38¢**

(Revenue)   (Production Costs)   (Profit)

The second incentive, a negative incentive, was that she risked losing her **CAPITAL**, the money (or other resources) used to start her business. Opportunity and risk are two factors that all entrepreneurs face.

Starting a business, even a lemonade stand, is always risky. Lori knew that she might go to all the trouble of painting a sign, squeezing lemons, buying cups, and setting up the table, only to find that nobody was thirsty enough to buy. But, she would be happy to do all this work *if* she made a good amount of money to put toward a new bike.

Lori's mom was willing to supply the sugar and water, but Lori would have to spend the money already saved for her bike to buy lemons and paper cups. This is money she would be **INVESTING** in her new business. An investment is a cost spent in hopes of making a **RETURN**, or a *future benefit*. Lori would be investing (spending money now) in hopes of making a return (receiving even more money in the future).

So before deciding to invest her own capital and take on the high workload, Lori did a cost-benefit analysis with number values to see if setting up a lemonade stand was something she was willing to do.

Costs of a lemonade stand
Could lose money already saved for bike [7]
Lots of work preparing lemonade [2]
Total Cost Value: 9

Benefits of a lemonade stand
Could make money for bike [5]
Satisfy thirst of others [5]
Total Benefit Value: 10

To Lori, the benefit of possible profit was high enough to justify the costs: all the work involved in making lemonade and setting up the stand, and the risk of maybe losing money.

Profit is usually a person's main incentive to produce goods and offer services to other people. Why would Mr. Goad go to all the expense and work of growing grapes if he couldn't make a profit? And why would Lori bother setting up a lemonade stand if *she* couldn't make a profit?

But is it *fair* to make a profit?

Lori's little brother Paul wasn't so sure. He thought Lori ought to charge him only the amount it cost her to produce the lemonade: 12 cents. "That would be more fair," he told Lori. "Why do you need to make a *profit* anyway?"

Paul hasn't yet learned that economic exchanges have to benefit *both* the buyer and the seller. Only when both sides benefit can the exchange be a moral one.

"Wait a minute, Paul," Lori shot back. "You benefit by drinking the lemonade. But if I don't make a profit, I don't benefit from our exchange. Is that fair?"

No, it isn't fair. It's only because people make profits that they can then pay their bills, buy things for their families, and produce more goods and services for their community.

Lori noticed, though, that other than her brother and her friend Wendy, nobody was buying her lemonade at 50 cents a glass. After a while, she decided to lower her price to 25 cents a glass because she knew that lowering the price increases the quantity demanded.

Lowering her price attracted more customers who were driving and walking by. Before long she had a group of people standing near her stand sipping lemonade and chatting about the latest neighborhood news. At the end of a very busy and fun day, Lori had earned $6.50 in profit to put toward her new bike!

Quick Quiz

Lesson 14

1. What do we call a person willing to accept the risks of starting a new business?
   a. capital
   b. entrepreneur
   c. profit

2. What was the specific risk, regarding her bike savings, that Lori was willing to take in starting a lemonade stand?

3. Profit equals _____ minus _____ .

4. What is the money called that people invest in businesses?

5. What is a "return" on an investment?

Section 3 Wrap-Up

Lesson 15

Think of an activity you'd like to try (scuba diving, learning Spanish, writing a book, etc.) and do a cost-benefit analysis to see if it's really worth doing. Try to consider things in your analysis like how much the activity will cost, how much work is involved, if it's safe, and how much you think you'll enjoy it. Remember to assign a number value to each cost and benefit.

My Activity: _____

Costs	Benefits
1.	1.
2.	2.
3.	3.
4.	4.
5.	5.

Total Cost Value: _____   Total Benefit Value: _____

Section 3 Wrap-Up, con't.

Lesson 15

If your costs are higher than your benefits, you may want to scrap the idea. However, if your total cost value is less than your total benefit value, this might be an activity worth trying! But **always** ask your parents first – they may know of some very important costs you hadn't considered.

Based on your number values, which was the most important incentive (positive or negative) in your cost-benefit analysis?

Section 3 Matching

Lesson 15

Match the following terms with the correct definitions:

Cost ☐   ☐ positive reward or motivation of behavior

Benefit ☐   ☐ comparing the pros and cons of a proposed action

Incentive ☐   ☐ opposite of benefit; a price or loss

Cost-benefit analysis ☐   ☐ money used to start a business

Entrepreneur ☐   ☐ opposite of cost: an advantage or gain

Capital ☐   ☐ a future benefit

Return on investment ☐   ☐ person accepting the risk of starting

The Friendship Market
Negotiating for limited resources
Section 4

Creating a Market

Lesson 16

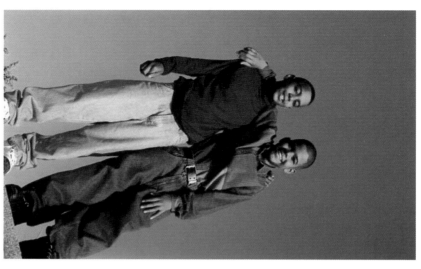

ANTHONY AND BOB HAVE BEEN best friends since the first grade. But today they're having an argument over how to spend their time. Anthony wants to watch a soccer game on TV. Bob wants to go swimming. How they resolve this argument can teach us a lot about economics.

Their friendship is like an economic **MARKET**. A market can be a store, a website, or any venue (setting) where buyers and sellers come together to **NEGOTIATE** exchanges. When two people negotiate, they discuss or argue or persuade until they come to an agreement.

So how is a friendship like a market? Instead of an exchange of goods, services, or assets, a friendship is an exchange of one's time, thoughts, problems, and joys for those of another.

Friendship, as a market, involves friends coming together and the interactions between them. They aren't buying or selling from one another, but they are making a series of negotiations based on their own costs and benefits and their incentives to treat the other person fairly.

So a market is any setting in which people negotiate exchanges, and where their actions are influenced by incentives.

Anthony and Bob have a strong friendship, and the desire to keep the friendship going is a powerful incentive. But their demands are still different, so they need to negotiate how they'll spend their time on Saturday afternoon. Anthony still wants to watch soccer, and Bob still wants to go swimming. They each want their own way, but friendship incentives push them to also consider what the other boy wants to do.

"Swimming is great exercise, Anthony," Bob reminds him. "And you want to be in good shape for the baseball game on Thursday."

"Yeah," Anthony says. "But these two soccer teams are only playing each other today, and we could swim tomorrow when the weather's supposed to be warmer."

After negotiating like this about which opportunity cost they're more willing to pay, they choose to do what Anthony wants today, and to do what Bob wants tomorrow. How do we know that what Anthony and Bob have chosen is fair? Because they've both *agreed*. There are friendship-market incentives at work, too. Each boy has the incentive of caring for his friend that motivates his behavior.

Of course, if too many of their negotiations seem unfair to Bob, he might end the friendship. But these boys have always negotiated well. As long as both feel the friendship benefits them, they have an incentive to treat one another fairly.

Quick Quiz

Lesson 16

1. What does it mean for two people to "negotiate"?

2. A market can be:
   a. a shop or store
   b. a friendship
   c. any setting for incentive-based negotiation of exchanges
   d. all of the above

3. How do we know that when Anthony and Bob negotiate how to spend their time, that their decision is fair?

4. What is the opportunity cost that Bob and Anthony will pay if they watch the soccer game?

Sharing Peanuts

TIME ISN'T MONEY, BUT WE still "spend" it. Choosing to spend it one way creates an opportunity cost – we must give up another way of "spending" our time. But why does this create an opportunity cost in the first place?

It's because time is a **RESOURCE**, a tool we use for our benefit. And like all resources in the world, it's **LIMITED**. That means there's *not* an endless supply. Money is also a **LIMITED RESOURCE** – it can be used up. None of our resources are unlimited; all of them are available in specific amounts.

Because our resources are limited, we must make choices about how to use them. This is why sharing is sometimes hard – when we share things with others, we're giving up some of our own limited resources.

Bob and Anthony have been swimming at Large Lake. After they get out, dry off, and get dressed, Bob buys a bag of peanuts. Anthony is a little hungry and hasn't brought any money, so he asks Bob if he'll share.

Now, Bob only has one bag of peanuts. If he had unlimited peanuts, choosing to share with Anthony wouldn't be a big deal. But he only has one bag – that's his limit today. So any peanuts he gives Anthony are peanuts he won't get to eat himself.

But Bob also has a powerful incentive to share with Anthony: he's a good friend. Bob wants to preserve the friendship, and he cares about Anthony – he doesn't want him to be hungry this afternoon. These incentives outweigh the costs to Bob, and he willingly chooses to share his limited amount of peanuts with Anthony.

Mr. Greedy L. McMeanie

Mr. Greedy L. McMeanie doesn't understand free markets. He hates to share. Mostly, he hates to share his profits with his employees. He only pays them to keep them from quitting. What if he used the power of sharing and kindness to motivate his employees? They'd have incentives to give back. If the brain of every person in McMeanie's company cared about that company, think of what they could accomplish together! That's the power of sharing your limited resources: your time, your money, your hard work, your ideas. People can move ahead farther and faster when they share their limited resources! Until Mr. McMeanie learns the power of sharing, his company will be slow to profit.

66

Quick Quiz

Lesson 17

1. When we have a "limited resource," it means that:

   a. we can have all we want

   b. there's none left

   c. we have *some*

2. Can limited resources be used up, or do they supply us forever?

3. Why is sharing sometimes hard to do?

Friends are Limited Resources

TAMMY AND ERIN HAVE BEEN good friends since preschool. And like Anthony and Bob, these girls create a market (a setting for negotiation) whenever they get together.

Two weeks ago, Tammy borrowed one of Erin's CDs, and now she's lost it. Now, Tammy's afraid to tell Erin – she knows that Erin will be mad. Maybe she could avoid making her angry by telling Erin a lie. "I'll just say my brother lost it," Tammy thinks. "That'll be easier."

Tammy has one incentive to lie but many incentives to tell the truth. One is that Erin is her friend and she cares about her. It would hurt Tammy to lie to her friend, and the pain she would feel is another cost. Not to mention that if Erin ever found out Tammy lied, Erin would be hurt and angry. That's more pain that would be a cost to Tammy. Finally, she could lose the friendship – a very high cost, indeed.

She decides the costs of lying to Erin far outweigh the benefit, so she keeps thinking. Probably the right thing to do, she realizes, is to buy Erin a new CD to replace the one she lost. This will be a monetary (money) cost to Tammy, and she only has so much money. Her money, like everyone else's, is a limited resource. Still, the cost of a new CD is much *lower* than the cost of losing her best friend. She chooses to replace it.

But it's still a choice. If Tammy didn't care about being a good friend and didn't respond to friendship-based incentives, she could value her limited resources – her money – more than she values Erin.

Even friends are limited resources – when we find a friend we all have very high incentives to keep that friend. And the markets we create when coming together with friends (the settings of negotiation with built-in incentives) help to keep us honest with one another.

But what about people with more resources than us? Do they experience economics or friendships differently? Money and the things we buy with money (like peanuts and CDs) are all limited resources. The same is true for the resources of rich people and big companies!

Phil Hughes owns a nation-wide lumber company. Lumber is a resource used to build houses. Lumber comes from trees and trees are limited. So Mr. Hughes doesn't escape the limitation of resources, no matter how rich he might be.

He also doesn't escape the market he creates when coming together with a friend. He still has incentives to treat his friend honestly and kindly, no matter how many resources he might have. He realizes, like Tammy, that our friends are limited resources and we must protect our friendships like we protect our assets.

Quick Quiz

Lesson 18

1. When we create a friendship market with someone, what's an incentive within that market that helps to keep us honest?

2. Why are friends limited resources?

3. True or False: A rich person, with more resources than a poor person, still has incentives to treat a poor person with honesty, respect, and kindness.

4. Do big corporations have to make choices based on limited resources?

Section 4 Wrap-Up

Lesson 19

Jody and Ben

Jody and Ben are good friends. Following is a situation they experienced last week. Help them label their limited resources and negotiate through their disagreement.

Ben's mother has given him $50 to spend and he wants to visit an amusement park with Jody. He can only go on Monday because he works the rest of the week. But Jody doesn't get paid until Friday and she can't afford the amusement park's admission fee, much less the price of rides and snacks. On Monday, she would rather go to the beach for free and lay in the sun.

1. What are Jody's limited resources?

Section 4 Wrap-Up, con't.

Lesson 19

2. Does Ben have any limited resources?

3. How might Ben convince Jody to go to the amusement park?

4. How could Jody convince Ben to go to the beach?

Section 4 Matching

Lesson 19

Match the following terms with the correct definitions:

Venue ☐

☐ money or materials without an endless supply

Negotiate ☐

☐ setting for incentive-based negotiation of exchanges

Market ☐

☐ a setting or place

Limited resources ☐

☐ to argue, discuss, or persuade until you reach an agreement

Cost Benefit Jr.™

Face Off

A little friendly competition

Section 5

The Smith's Goldfish

Lesson 20

OVER THE SUMMER, NICHOLAS expanded his dog-walking service to include all forms of pet care. He's the most successful young entrepreneur on Lafayette Street. His pet-care business is doing so well, he doesn't have time for any new customers!

He now walks the Pruitt's dog as well as Mrs. Burton's dog. He feeds his aunt's parakeet whenever she's out of town. He even looked after Mr. Goad's chickens one week when the grape business got extremely busy. The only job Nicholas won't take is feeding the Smith's goldfish: he doesn't like fish.

Nicholas has been making about $25 a week caring for the pets of his relatives and neighbors. But one day last week he showed up to walk Mrs. Burton's poodle, Baby, and she told him at the door that she wouldn't need his services any longer.

He was shocked. "Why not?" he asked.

"There's another dog-walker who just came by. He offered to walk Baby for less money than you charge."

This other dog-walker turned out to be a second-grader named Todd. Nicholas had seen Todd around town riding his bike. And now he was approaching Nicholas' customers, charging less.... Todd was even willing to feed the Smith's goldfish! Nicholas realized what was happening; Todd was competing with him for the Lafayette Street pet-care business.

COMPETITION between two businesses means that both are trying to win over the same customers. Another word for customer is **CONSUMER**.

Competition is good for the consumer. It was good for Mrs. Burton; she got the same dog-walking service from Todd for less money than she had been paying Nicholas. When businesses compete, consumers win. This is because the best way to compete for a customer is to offer them more benefits or fewer costs than your competitor.

So, if Todd wants to compete with Nicholas for Mrs. Burton's business, he can offer her a lower price. That's what he's done, and Todd has been successful in his competition for some of Nicholas' business.

Mr. Greedy L. McMeanie

Mr. Greedy L. McMeanie doesn't like to compete; he would rather control. When other companies try to sell what he sells, but at lower prices, Mr. McMeanie doesn't lower his prices. Instead, he tries to buy out his competitors, run them out of business by telling lies about them in the community, or he has his friends on the City Council pass laws against his competitors. Still, success is a reward we all must compete for, even for Greedy L. McMeanie. Eventually, the marketplace will force him to compete for your business. Nobody can control their competitors, or their customers, for long. And success comes faster and easier when we allow competition to shape our business products and business behaviors into the best they can be.

Quick Quiz

Lesson 20

1. What's another word for "customer"?

2. When businesses compete, they're trying to win over **THE SAME / DIFFERENT** consumers. (circle one)

3. Who benefits most from the competition between businesses?

4. What do you think Nicholas could do to win back some of the customers he lost to Todd?

The Babysitter Wars

Lesson 21

MR. DAVIS AND MR. ROBINSON are golfing buddies. Their families are friends; even their kids play together at the city park. But there is one thing that causes these good friends to compete ruthlessly with one another: the coolest babysitter in town – Allison Carter.

Mr. Davis' son Ryan cries if his parents call any other babysitter. Mr. Robinson's daughter Lisa loves Allison; she's the only babysitter able to make Lisa laugh when her parents leave. In fact, most children in town think she's the best babysitter there is. She's more fun than cartoons, board games, or french fries.

The competition between these two dads all started when the Davis family and the Robinson family both needed a sitter on Friday night. Of course, both called Allison and she could only accept one job. As it happened, she chose to babysit that night for the Robinsons because they were willing to pay her $2 an hour – a higher wage than she usually got.

When Mr. Davis found out, he called Allison back and offered to pay her $2.50 an hour. He was competing for Allison, but not for Allison-the-consumer. He was competing for Allison-the-worker. Employers often compete for workers who they feel do a good job.

So while a business can compete with other businesses to win over consumers, an **EMPLOYER** (a person or company who hires others to do jobs) can compete with other employers to win over workers. Like businesses competing for consumers, employers often try to win over workers by competing for consumers, employers often try to win over workers by offering them <u>more benefits</u> than their competitors offer.

A higher wage, a pleasant working environment, or health insurance are all examples of benefits employers might offer to workers they want to hire. The worker can then pick the job with the most benefits. These benefits work as *incentives* to motivate the worker to accept the job, and to perform well at their job.

That Friday night, Allison had to say no to Mr. Davis because she had already made a commitment to Mr. Robinson. But she did remember the offer Mr. Davis made. And the next week, when both dads again called, asking her to baby-sit, she chose Mr. Davis and *his* higher wage.

Quick Quiz

Lesson 21

1. What is an employer?

2. Why would an employer compete for a certain worker?

3. An employer competing for a good worker might offer:
   a. the incentive of a higher wage
   b. the incentive of a pleasant working environment
   c. the incentive of health insurance
   d. any of the above

4. Competition for a worker is similar to competition for a consumer because both forms of competition involve offering more _____ and fewer _____ than your competitor does.

Mr. Blue and the Red Canoe

Lesson 22

FOR THEIR 40th WEDDING anniversary, Mr. Blue was planning to take his wife to Large Lake on vacation. They would stay in a cozy log cabin and go fishing, paddling, and hiking. But before they could leave on the trip, Mr. Blue needed to get them a new boat.

So on Saturday morning, he went down to the **AUCTION** house. An auction is a marketplace where all sorts of people, like Mr. Blue, BID on items that are up for sale.

When people bid a certain price, they're showing a willingness to buy the item at that price. But another person can offer a higher bid, if that person is willing to pay more. The bidding continues until the price goes so high, most bidders are unwilling to pay it. So rather than *businesses* competing for *consumers*, the auction lets consumers compete for the *goods*.

Mr. Blue got down to the auction house early on Saturday morning. There was a bright red canoe, newly painted, going up for sale and he wanted a chance to see the boat up close before the bidding started. The canoe was in good condition and he decided to bid for it. But Mr. Blue only had $200 to spend.

When the auction started, the auctioneer called out an opening bid of $85. A tall man in black boots lifted his sign to indicate he was willing to buy the canoe for that price. Since someone was willing to spend $85, the auctioneer called out a higher price, "$90?" Mr. Blue raised *his* sign.

The bidding went back and forth until Mr. Blue was the last bidder to raise his sign. He had responded to a bid of $175. When the auctioneer called out "$180?" to see if the man in black boots was willing to go that high, the man shook his head and kept his sign in his lap.

"$175 then... going once... going twice... sold to Mr. Blue!"

After the bidding was over, the tall man in black boots came over. "Congratulations – nice little boat. What do you plan to do with her?" Mr. Blue told him about the anniversary trip to the lake, and the two men shook hands.

Just because they had been competing against one another for the boat didn't mean they had bad feelings. Competition is a natural way for people to sort out life's highest bidders – those who value the world's various limited resources the most.

Mr. and Mrs. Blue took their new red canoe to the lake on their anniversary. They paddled, floated, sipped coffee on the rocks, and watched the sun set over the mountain. It was a very happy day.

Quick Quiz

Lesson 22

1. Who is competing for what at an auction?

2. What does it mean when a person makes a "bid" at an auction?

3. When people compete for products, workers, or consumers, are they being mean or unfair to one another?

4. Can you list some other ways people compete?

Section 5 Wrap-Up

Lesson 23

A GAME OF STORE

Ask some friends to play a game of Store. Two people will each own stores – they should both gather 10 to 15 items from around the house to "sell." Each storeowner is responsible for setting the prices of their products. The rest of the people playing (your parents or other friends) will "shop" at the two stores with the play money provided on the next few pages. Each shopper gets only $8, so storeowners shouldn't price their products too high.

The object of the game is to convince shoppers to buy from your store rather than your opponent's. You can persuade them not only by choosing good items to sell, but also by selling them at fair, even *competitive* prices. The first person to earn $9 wins!

Remember, if you don't win at a certain game, you might find that your loss is an *incentive* to play better next time, to learn better strategies, or to find another game or activity that you're better at doing. Businesses and employers also find that losing can be an incentive to charge better prices or offer better wages in the future. So losing a game, or a competition, isn't always a bad thing! We learn a lot when we lose.

After you play the game of Store, answer the following questions:

1. How did you compete with your opponent to draw customers?

Section 5 Wrap-Up, con't.

Lesson 23

2. If you lowered your prices to compete in the game, were you trying to increase demand or quantity demanded?

3. If you're trying to win by competing, does that mean you dislike your opponent?

4. Winning is great, but if you lost, that's OK -- do you know why?

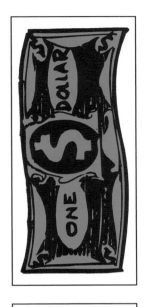
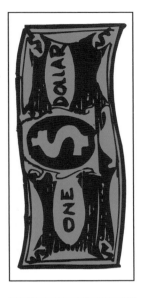
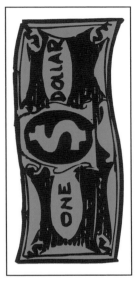

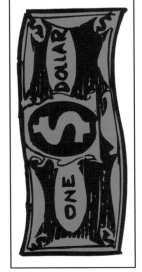

Cost Benefit Jr.™

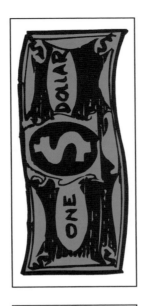

Cost Benefit Jr.™

Section 5 Matching

Lesson 23

Match the following terms with the correct definitions:

Competition ☐   ☐ buyer of goods or services; customer

Consumer ☐   ☐ person or company who hires workers

Employer ☐   ☐ an offer to pay a certain price for an item

Auction ☐   ☐ two people trying to obtain the same resource

Bid ☐   ☐ marketplace where buyers bid on goods

Cost Benefit Jr.™

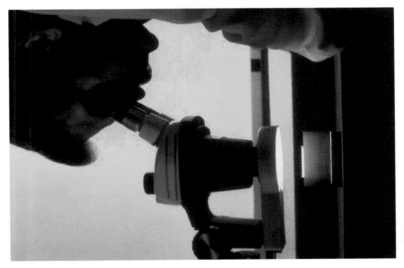

The Unseen

Hidden costs & benefits

Section 6

Cory's Friends

Lesson 24

CORY JUST BOUGHT A NEW motorcycle. It's shiny, runs well, looks expensive, and he's showing it off all around town. Cory's friends certainly can't afford a motorcycle like this – or any motorcycle, for that matter! They're still walking wherever they go, and their new favorite topic of conversation is Cory and his motorcycle.

In fact, most of Cory's friends are feeling jealous. After all, why should Cory have it so good? Sure, he worked at the grocery store after school bagging groceries. But most of his friends have similar jobs, and they could never afford a bike like that.

Some of Cory's friends think his grandparents bought the bike for him. Some of them think it was probably just cheap. Whatever the case, his friends are jealous because it seems Cory doesn't deserve this benefit.

What Cory's friends *don't see*, though, is all the extra work he did, and all the things Cory gave up to save for his motorcycle.

They don't realize, for example, that Cory worked extra jobs. They only saw him at his grocery store job – they weren't there when he shoveled driveways in the winter and weeded gardens and mowed lawns in the summer.

When they see Cory cleaning and polishing his motorcycle, they don't see that he gave up playing on the football team so he could work those jobs. They don't see that last year he rarely went to the movies with his girlfriend, Beth. They don't see the trip to Florida he chose to pass up during spring break.

And since the trip to Florida was the next-best option he could have chosen (rather than his motorcycle), the trip to Florida was his **OPPORTUNITY COST**.

Cory's friends *chose* to spend much of their wages on nights out bowling or playing pinball. Every fun activity his friends did without him was a cost Cory was willing to pay – costs his friends were *not* willing to pay – in order to buy his motorcycle.

Mr. Greedy L. McMeanie

Mr. Greedy L. McMeanie doesn't understand free markets because of what he just doesn't see. He doesn't see that bad business practices eventually kill profits. He doesn't see that if your customers don't trust you, you'll lose your share of the market. He doesn't see that higher prices decrease the quantity of his products that are demanded! That's the power of knowledge in a free market: without knowledge of what you can see and what you can't see, you can't succeed economically. Mr. McMeanie needs to put on the glasses of economic knowledge!

Quick Quiz

Lesson 24

1. Since an opportunity cost is usually something not done, an action not taken, is an opportunity cost something we can always see?

2. What was the opportunity cost Cory paid for choosing the motorcycle?

3. Do you think his friends would feel less jealous if they could see everything Cory gave up for his motorcycle?

4. Should we be jealous of the benefits other people have? Why?

Dave Gives Up a Sale

Lesson 25

BEFORE LONG, THE ENGINE in Cory's new motorcycle started to make a funny sound. He was worried and decided to take it down to Dave's Auto Shop.

"Can you take a look at this, Dave?" he asked. The mechanic was happy to help. He'd known Cory's family a long time and they were good customers.

Dave saw that it wasn't a serious problem. The engine just needed a tune-up. He could make about $200 tuning it up, but he knew that Cory would want to do the job himself, to learn more about motorcycle engines and to save money. So he didn't charge Cory for looking at the engine and didn't ask for the business of the tune-up. He gave up the $200 sale.

John works with Dave and he can't understand why Dave would give up a job that would easily earn $200. What John *doesn't* see are the benefits that will come as a result of giving up Cory's tune-up.

In fact, that same day Cory told his mother about how helpful Dave had been. His mother was having Mrs. Burton over for tea – she was the lady who owned the poodle down the street. She heard the whole story and was impressed.

The following week, Mrs. Burton's nephew was looking for a good auto repair shop, and she remembered Cory's experience at Dave's. So Mrs. Burton referred her nephew to Dave.

Six months later, Mrs. Burton's car broke down and she then took *her* business to Dave, too. In fact, over the next year, a total of seven new customers were referred to Dave because of his helpfulness to Cory. These seven customers came in at different times of the year and never mentioned Cory, but it was from giving up that $200 sale that all this new business came!

Dave's opportunity cost was much more visible to John than the benefits that followed. This is because they didn't happen immediately – they would happen later, spread out over time. Remember: when we pay a cost now in hopes of gaining *future* benefits, we're making an investment. So Dave's helpfulness to Cory wasn't just a nice thing to do – it was an investment in Dave's future business.

Still, investments are risky – they don't always make a return. Dave knows that not every helpful action toward his customers will bring in new business. But Dave can make his own choices about which risks he's willing to take.

Quick Quiz

Lesson 24

1. Dave's seven new customers are an example of unseen **COSTS / BENEFITS.** (circle one)

2. One reason Dave's new customer benefits are unseen is that they happen:
   a. in the dark
   b. in the future
   c. in another city

3. Because Dave gave up a sale in order to gain a future benefit, we can call that an
   _____.

4. Do investments always make a return?

Linda's Lost Sale

EMILY IS MRS. BURTON'S

neighbor, and today *she* needs to find a good auto repair shop. Emily has backed into a fence, breaking her taillight and smashing her bumper. Mrs. Burton is happy to give Dave's number to Emily.

She sees that Emily's having a bad day, so Mrs. Burton tries to cheer her up. "Don't worry, dear," she says, patting Emily on the shoulder. "At least that nice mechanic Dave will get some unexpected business today. It'll be good for the town's economy!"

But Mrs. Burton is only half right. It is good for Dave to get business, but Emily's broken fender will <u>not</u> improve the economy of the town as a whole.

What Mrs. Burton *doesn't see* is that when Emily backed into the fence, she was on her way to see Linda Strauss, who makes beautiful pottery. Emily had planned to buy several pots from Linda to decorate a room in her home. But because she's spending $200 on car repairs (money going to Dave) she can't spend $200 on pottery (money that would have gone to Linda). Linda has lost a sale.

Emily's smashed fender doesn't improve the town's economy – it doesn't *create* a new sale. It just **DIVERTS**, or moves, Linda's sale over to Dave.

Now, Emily never intended to pay money to Dave, the mechanic, today. So is this economic exchange really based on Emily's freedom to make choices – is the exchange a moral one? Isn't Emily being "forced" to repair her car? It certainly wasn't her choice to hit the fence!

Remember, it was Emily's own action that caused the accident. She was *responsible* for it, whether she would have chosen it or not. She's also making the *choice* to have her car fixed; she could choose, instead, to just drive the car around town with a broken bumper. So, yes, it's a moral exchange – it's based on her freedom to make choices. We must see that fixing her car is a choice, whether she *enjoys* making that choice, or not.

Quick Quiz

Lesson 26

1. Why wasn't Emily's car accident helpful to the town's economy?

2. Who was responsible for Emily's car accident?

3. What was the opportunity cost Emily paid when she decided to fix the dent in her fender?

4. Even though she didn't choose to have an accident, was her economic exchange with Dave a moral one?

Section 6 Wrap-Up

Lesson 27

Write a short story about a girl or boy who wins a sporting championship. Be sure to include details about the sport, how they won, and who supported them. Then, end the story describing an unseen cost the character has paid, or an unseen benefit they receive.

Lesson 27

Section 6 Wrap-Up, con't.

Section 6 Matching

Lesson 27

Match the following terms with the correct definitions:

Unseen ☐

☐ next-best option we give up when we make a choice

Benefit ☐

☐ cost paid now in order to gain a future benefit

Opportunity Cost ☐

☐ sale sent in another direction

Investment ☐

☐ not visible or obvious to the community

Diverted Sale ☐

☐ opposite of cost: an advantage or gain

Cost Benefit Jr.™

Food Economics

The basics of saving and consumption

Section 7

Candy vs. Carrot

Lesson 28

SOUNDRA HAS TROUBLE WITH A CERTAIN group of foods called "carbohydrates." This type of food includes sweets, like cake, cookies and candy, and plants like fruits, vegetables and grains. Carbohydrates join fats and proteins as the three types of food we all eat.

Not everyone watches "carbs" just to lose weight. For Soundra, too many carbs can affect her body's blood sugar levels. So Soundra's nutritionist has asked her to limit her carbs. At each meal, Soundra eats only 50 grams of carbohydrates. If she eats less than 50 at a meal, she can have dessert.

Today for lunch, Soundra's mother has made turkey sandwiches, chips, carrots, and milk. The sandwich has about 20 grams of carbs; the chips, carrots and milk all have about 10 grams each, per serving. This lunch totals 50 carb grams.

Soundra enjoys the sandwich and she loves the chips, but she knows that eating the carrots (not her favorite vegetable) will prevent her from eating any candy after lunch. One serving of carrots has about the same number of carbohydrate grams as three chocolate kisses, so eating carrots has an opportunity cost of three chocolate kisses.

Soundra's mother would never allow her to skip carrots in order to eat chocolate. That's because carrots are more nutritious than chocolate. The benefits of eating carrots include beta-carotene (which our bodies turn into vitamin A), potassium, vitamin C, and a type of fiber called calcium pectate. The benefit of eating chocolate is mainly taste.

There are also costs for eating both foods. Remember, carrots have an opportunity cost of three chocolate kisses. Soundra is tempted to choose taste over vitamins, minerals, and fiber, which is not a choice we should make very often.

When we eat, we **CONSUME** food. When we buy things, we **CONSUME** goods. Consumption happens, then, when we buy, eat or use a resource that cannot then be bought, eaten or used by another person.

If Soundra consumes carrots at lunch, she prevents her own consumption of chocolate. Consumption is important to both our health (through eating) and our economy (through spending), but consumption always requires us to make choices and be very aware of our opportunity costs.

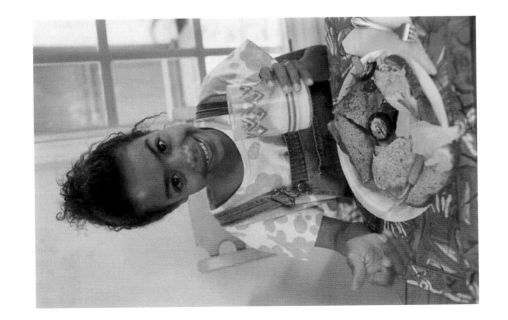

Soundra wisely decides to take the benefit of nutrition over the benefit of taste and chooses to consume her carrots at the expense of the chocolate. But she asks her mom to make sirloin steak and a green salad with a roll for dinner, which add up to only about 25 carb grams. She'll then save 25 grams for later by not "spending" or "consuming" them. After dinner, she can spend or consume those extra 25 grams on something yummy.

Mom is impressed by the choices Soundra made at lunch and agrees to make steak and salad. Because she's wisely **BUDGETED** her carbohydrate grams (planned to spend and save certain amounts) Soundra will be able to enjoy dessert tonight!

Quick Quiz

Lesson 28

1. What is Soundra's opportunity cost for choosing to eat a serving of carrots?

2. What are four benefits of eating carrots?

    1.

    2.

    3.

    4.

3. When we eat, we "consume" food, and when we buy things, we _____ goods.

4. Budgeting means:
    a. planning to spend (consume) and save a certain amount
    b. being a fuss-budget
    c. eating less

5. What can Soundra do to "save" carbohydrate grams?

The Marginal Utility Buffet

JULIE'S FAMILY HAS JUST BEEN to a fancy restaurant for brunch. They ate from a huge, scrumptious buffet and Julie loaded her plate more than once. She ate way too much food and now she has a tummy ache.

Why did Julie make this mistake? She forgot an important economic lesson!

Her first bite of blueberry waffle was magnificent, but do you think the last bite of her fourth waffle was just as magnificent? Probably not. By then she was very full and somewhat sick of the taste of blueberry waffles. The first bite is usually more satisfying to us than any later bite, and that's true in economics, too.

Remember that *utility* is the satisfaction of a want or need. So every time we consume an additional bite of waffle, we experience additional satisfaction. The additional satisfaction we get from each additional bite is our **MARGINAL UTILITY.**

Now, Julie's first bite of waffle might have given her a satisfaction level of 10. Her last bite, though, only gave her a satisfaction level of 2. With each bite, she experienced less and less marginal utility. When additional waffle bites give us smaller and smaller amounts of satisfaction, we experience **DIMINISHING MARGINAL UTILITY.**

112

Julie certainly experienced diminishing marginal utility at the buffet! Still, she *chose* to eat all that food, and she was harmed by her own choices.

Did she mean to harm herself? Of course not! She made her choices by looking only at the benefits (like the good taste of the food), and not at the costs. Over time, eating too much of the wrong foods can give us more than a tummy-ache. It can cause a fat body or even a disease called diabetes. We need to be aware of these costs, rather than just looking at the benefits of taste.

There were other costs, too. Julie was planning to fly kites in the park after the brunch, but now she feels too sick to go. Over-eating at the buffet had a cost she hadn't foreseen: giving up flying kites.

Julie has learned two important lessons: 1) that too much food brings diminishing marginal utility, and 2) that she should make choices that will benefit her *more* than they cost her. The next time her family goes to a nice restaurant, Julie will remember these lessons and will budget her food amounts. Then she'll be free to play, and feel good doing it, when the meal is over.

Mr. Greedy L. McMeanie

Mr. Greedy L. McMeanie grows fatter and fatter because he doesn't know how to plan what to consume and what to save. He behaves this way with both his money and his food. He doesn't worry about budgets with money because, if he overspends, he'll just try to overcharge his customers. But what about his food intake? If he overspends by eating too much, what can he do? Who can he overcharge then? Mr. McMeanie won't be healthy physically or economically until he learns to plan, save, and budget. Once he learns how to do that, he won't have to try cheating other people to get ahead. And he can stop cheating himself, too!

Quick Quiz

Lesson 29

1. When a product satisfies a want or a need, that's called:
   a. utility
   b. marginal utility
   c. diminishing marginal utility

2. The additional amount of satisfaction from each additional unit of a product is called:
   a. utility
   b. marginal utility
   c. diminishing marginal utility

3. When each additional unit of a product gives us a smaller amount of additional satisfaction, that's called:
   a. utility
   b. marginal utility
   c. diminishing marginal utility

The Gain in Loss

Lesson 30

MRS. BURTON HAS DECIDED to get in shape. She's been exercising and watching what she eats. She keeps her calories, fats, carbohydrates, and proteins in balance. These are expressed in number values, so it's easy to budget her food.

A few months ago, she made a plan – a budget – to keep her meals under 1200 calories per day, her carb grams under 100, her protein grams around 80, and fat under 80 grams per day.

She kept within her budgeted calories and food grams by staying away from certain foods like desserts, pizza, and greasy french fries, while eating more salads, raw vegetables, and lean meats.

In addition to her food budget, Mrs. Burton started exercising. It's good for her bones and her heart, and a 30-minute workout on the stationary bicycle can burn off about 200 calories. That's about 17 **PERCENT** (%) of her daily allowance of calories.

A **PERCENTAGE** means "per 100." So 25% is 25 "per 100." If you have $100 in the bank and you withdraw $25, that's 25 out of 100. You've taken 25% of your total.

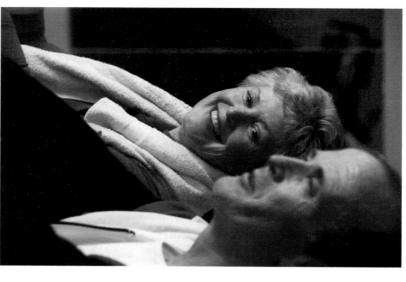

An easy way to figure a percentage is to <u>divide the piece by the whole</u>. If you save $30 and buy a DVD for $15, what percentage of your savings have you spent?

15 (the piece) divided by 30 (the whole) = .50 or 50%

Percentages are just fractions of the whole, and they can also be expressed with a decimal point:

.35 = 35%

Over a few months of budgeting and calculating her daily percentages, Mrs. Burton has lost 10 pounds! Now, we may not be used to a negative number representing a gain, but Mrs. Burton's loss of 10 pounds *is* a gain – a benefit resulting from exercising and food budgeting!

Quick Quiz

Lesson 30

1. How can budgeting help Mrs. Burton lose weight?

2. The word "percentage" means "per _____."

3. When we have 50%, how many out of 100 do we have?

4. What's an easy way to calculate a percentage? (Use the words "piece" and "whole" in your answer.)

5. How do we express 50% with a decimal point?

Section 7 Wrap-Up

Lesson 31

Let's do a cost-benefit analysis on the consumption of certain foods, including asparagus, eggs and apple pie. Following are the nutrition labels you'll need to put these analyses together.

Nutrition Facts

Serving Size 1/2 cup (90 g)

Amount Per Serving

Calories 22

	% Daily Value
Total Fat 0.3 g	0%
Saturated Fat 0.1 g	0%
Cholesterol 0 mg	0%
Sodium 10 mg	0%
Total Carbohydrate 4 g	1%
Dietary Fiber 1.5 g	1%
Sugars 2.5 g	
Protein 2 g	

Nutrition Facts

Serving Size 1 egg (50 g)

Amount Per Serving

Calories 74

	% Daily Value
Total Fat 5 g	15%
Saturated Fat 1.6 g	16%
Cholesterol 212 mg	140%
Sodium 63 mg	5%
Total Carbohydrate .5 g	0%
Dietary Fiber 0 g	0%
Sugars .5 g	
Protein 6 g	

Nutrition Facts

Serving Size 1 piece (110 g)

Amount Per Serving

Calories 290

	% Daily Value
Total Fat 13 g	18%
Saturated Fat 6 g	26%
Cholesterol 9 mg	3%
Sodium 350 mg	12%
Total Carbohydrate 41 g	12%
Dietary Fiber 1 g	0%
Sugars 40 g	
Protein 3 g	

Section 7 Wrap-Up, con't.

Lesson 31

Asparagus Costs

Fat _____

Sugars _____

Total: _____

Egg Costs

Fat _____

Sugars _____

Total: _____

Apple Pie Costs

Fat _____

Sugars _____

Total: _____

Asparagus Benefits

Fiber _____

Protein _____

Total: _____

Egg Benefits

Fiber _____

Protein _____

Total: _____

Apple Pie Benefits

Fiber _____

Protein _____

Total: _____

119

Section 7 Wrap-Up, con't.

Lesson 31

1. Based on an analysis of these four factors (fat, sugars, fiber, and protein), which food has the highest benefits?

2. Which food has the lowest costs?

3. To pick a winner, subtract the **COSTS [C]** from the **BENEFITS [B]**:

Asparagus	Eggs	Apple Pie
B — C	B — C	B — C
— — = —	— — = —	— — = —

4. Which food is the winner?

Section 7 Matching

Lesson 31

Match the following terms with the correct definitions:

Consumption ☐   ☐ a plan to consume and save specific amounts

Savings ☐   ☐ to spend or use a resource

Marginal Utility ☐   ☐ resources not consumed

Budget ☐   ☐ fractional amount per 100

Percentage ☐   ☐ satisfaction from additional consumption

121

Cost Benefit Jr.™

Money Flow

How money circulates in an economy

Section 8

Buying Helps the Flow

Lesson 32

ECONOMIES, LIKE MARKETS, are everywhere. A town has an economy, and it's part of the larger economies of the county, state, and nation. Economies are the interactions between those who produce and sell goods and services (like Mr. Goad, Dave the mechanic, or Allison the babysitter) and consumers (like Keira, Cory, and Mr. Blue). All these people, along with their jobs, their money, their choices, their products, and their ideas, make up the town's economy. An economy, then, is *a system of production and consumption.*

Every economy, big or small, is like a river. The money in the economy tends to flow through it like water. This is a very visible thing.

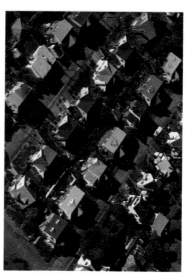

So how does money flow through an economy? The most obvious way is through consumption – people buying things. When people buy Mr. Goad's grapes, their money moves. When Mr. Goad gets his car fixed at Dave's auto shop, that money moves again. When Dave pays Allison to baby-sit his children, that money moves again.

With that same money, Allison can shop at the outdoor market with her sister, Heidi. Today, she's buying a pair of sandals from Mr. Weir, a market **VENDOR**. Vendor is another word for "seller."

Consumption, then, is one way money flows through an economy.

Quick Quiz

Lesson 32

1. What is an economy?

2. What does money tend to do in an economy?

3. What's the most obvious, visible way that money flows through an economy?

4. What do vendors do?

Investing Helps the Flow

Lesson 33

CONSUMPTION IS GOOD FOR

money flow, but people don't want to spend all their money just to keep the economy healthy – they'd go broke! Instead, smart consumers try to save some of their money.

Why do they save? One reason is diminishing marginal utility! Because many products give us less and less satisfaction as we consume more and more units, we have an incentive to consume less and save more.

Investing is another way to keep money flowing through the economy. But while consumption flow is visible to people, investment flow is usually *unseen*.

For example, many people keep their savings in a **BANK**. A bank is a place where people *store* their money. Every week Mr. Goad brings part of the profit he's made selling grapes to the bank. That money then becomes a **DEPOSIT** (money placed in a bank). He makes his deposits in a savings account. One benefit to Mr. Goad is that the bank can keep his money safe – it won't be stolen or lost, as it could be if he kept it at home. Another benefit is that the bank may pay **INTEREST** on his deposit. Interest is a fee paid for borrowing money.

This is one way to invest money, but any situation where you give your money to be used by someone else and in hopes of a larger return is an investment. The cost you pay for the benefit of a larger return is that you won't have your money while it's invested; someone else will be using it.

Quick Quiz

Lesson 33

1. What is an "interest" payment?

2. When we place our money in a bank, it's called a:

   a. profit
   b. deposit
   c. loan

3. Does saving money still allow it to flow through an economy?

Hoarding Helps the Flow, Too

BY NOW, KEIRA UNDERSTANDS A LOT about economics, and she worries that her allowance (which she still keeps in her piggy bank) isn't part of the economic flow. She wonders if she should put her allowance money in a savings account down at the bank so it can flow through the economy.

Keeping her money in the bank, however, will create an opportunity cost: Keira won't be able to spend the money while it's in the savings account. She's not sure that she's willing to pay that particular opportunity cost, especially for an amount of money so small. Who wants to go to the bank every time you want to buy a candy bar?

She would rather just keep her allowance where it is, in her room. But does her piggy bank hurt the economy by keeping her money out of the flow? Keira decided to ask her dad.

He was glad she asked, and assured Keira that keeping her money in a piggy bank, under a mattress, or even buried in the back yard, doesn't hurt the economy at all. In fact, **HOARDING** money (storing it somewhere safely hidden) actually helps everyone in an economy.

To see why, let's look at socks. Imagine you owned only one pair of socks. You would probably care much more about that pair than you have ever cared about socks before. If you lost one of those socks, your feet would suffer. Wearing shoes without socks can hurt, and in the winter your toes would freeze!

SOCKS!

If I own:	I might value one pair at this level:
1 pair	100
5 pairs	20
10 pairs	10
20 pairs	5

When you only have one pair of socks, that pair becomes much more valuable to you than if you had 20 pairs of socks. We can show this with number values:

Now, let's say you have 10 pairs of socks. If someone increases your supply of socks to 20 pairs, the value of each pair of socks you own will fall (in this case, from a value of 10 to a value of 5). And if someone decreased your supply of socks, each pair you still had would become more valuable to you.

It works the same way with money. If you decrease the supply of dollars in the economy by hoarding some in a piggy bank, you make all the other dollars left in the economy more valuable. If enough people in an economy hoard cash, they can actually raise the value of the dollar and increase their purchasing power. When each dollar is worth more, you can purchase more with those dollars.

Her dad wanted Keira to understand that it's just fine to keep her allowance in a piggy bank. In a free market, it's her choice what action to take with her money, whether that's spending it, saving/investing it, or even stashing it away.

Quick Quiz

Lesson 34

1. What are the three things we can do with our money?

    1.

    2.

    3.

2. What does "hoard" mean?

3. Does hoarding money hurt the economy? Why or why not?

Section 8 Wrap-Up

Lesson 35

How much interest can a person earn by keeping money in a bank's savings account?
Let's calculate the percentage at Keira's hometown bank.

First National Bank pays 2%

In the chart below, input your weekly allowance in the first column. Multiply that by 52 (there are 52 weeks in a year) to calculate your yearly income. (Income is another word for "revenue.") To find 30% of that, multiply your yearly income by .30. (Multiply by .60 when saving 60%.) This number is the amount of your yearly savings. Multiply your savings by .02 to calculate your 2% annual (yearly) return.

If your weekly allowance is:	Your yearly income is:	If you save 30%, your savings is:	Your yearly 2% interest is:
$1.50	$78.00	$23.40	$0.47
$2.00			
$3.00			

Section 8 Wrap-Up, con't.

Lesson 35

If your weekly allowance is:	Your yearly income is:	If you save 60%, your savings is:	Your yearly 2% interest is:
$1.50	$78.00	$46.80	$0.94
$2.00	_____	_____	_____
$3.00	_____	_____	_____

Phil Hughes, the owner of a nation-wide lumber company, has a savings account at First National Bank earning 2% interest. His weekly salary is $3750 and he saves 20% of that. How much interest does Phil Hughes make in a year?

If his weekly salary is:	His yearly income is:	If he saves 20%, his savings is:	His yearly 2% interest is:
$3750	_____	_____	_____

Section 8 Matching

Lesson 35

Match the following terms with the correct definitions:

Vendor ☐   ☐ revenue; money coming "in"

Income ☐   ☐ money placed in a bank

Deposit ☐   ☐ to safely store away

Interest ☐   ☐ seller

Hoard ☐   ☐ fee for borrowing money

Glossary

allowance
1. payment kids receive for doing chores;
2. percentage of a budget "allowable" to spend

asset
something you own

auction
marketplace where buyers bid on goods

bank
financial institution that pays interest on deposits, *charges interest* on loans, and keeps money safe

barter
trading goods without money

benefit
opposite of cost: an advantage or gain

bid
offering to pay or charge a certain price

budget
a plan to spend and save specific amounts

business
1. a company, corporation, or firm;
2. work done to make profits

buyer
someone who buys goods or services; see consumer, customer

capital
money used to invest in a business

choice
selection based on costs and benefits

competition
two or more people trying to obtain the same resource

consumer
someone who buys goods or services; see buyer, customer

consumption
to spend or use a resource

cost — opposite of benefit; a price or loss

cost-benefit analysis — comparing the pros and cons of a proposed action

customer — someone who buys goods or services; see buyer, consumer

demand — consumers' willingness and ability to buy

deposit — money placed in a bank

diminishing marginal utility — additional consumption giving less and less additional satisfaction

divert — send in another direction

earn — make money

economy — a system of production and consumption

employee — person working for another person or company

employer — person or company who hires workers

entrepreneur — person who accepts the risk of starting a business

exchange — giving and receiving

expense — cost

fair price — price agreed upon by sellers and buyers

freedom — independence; the absence of force or outside control

goods — tangible products that satisfy people's wants and needs

hoard — to safely store something away

incentive — positive reward or motivation of behavior

income — revenue; money coming "in"

intangible — something you cannot touch or hold

interest — fee paid for borrowing money

investment — cost paid now in order to gain a future benefit

limited resource — tools or materials without an endless supply

loan — borrowed money

marginal utility — additional consumption giving additional satisfaction

market — setting for incentive-based negotiation of exchanges

monetary — pertaining to money

negotiate — argue, discuss, or persuade until agreement is reached

opportunity cost — next-best option given up when we make a choice

percentage — a fractional amount per 100; the piece divided by the whole

price — payment required to buy goods or services

Stories in Microeconomics

production — work that has value to others

production cost — cost of producing goods and services

profit — revenue minus production costs

resource — tool or material used for our benefit

return — future benefit of investment

revenue — money received when selling goods or services

savings — money not spent

savings account — money deposited in a bank that earns interest

scarcity — see "limited resources"

seller — person charging a price in exchange for goods or services

services — intangible products that satisfy people's wants and needs

spend — to use or consume

subjective value — value that varies from person to person

supply — goods or services a producer is willing and able to sell

tangible — something you can touch or hold

unseen benefit — positive economic result not visible to the community

unseen cost — negative economic result not visible to the community

141

utility   satisfaction of a want or need

value   1. numerical amount;
            2. worth of goods or services

vendor   seller

voluntary   done without force

wage   money paid for work done

worker   employee; person who works